A PRIVATE ANTHOLOGY

UNIFORM WITH THIS VOLUME

A TREASURY OF ENGLISH PROSE FROM CHAUCER TO BERNARD SHAW

Compiled by LOGAN PEARSALL SMITH

A PRIVATE ANTHOLOGY

MADE BY

N. G. ROYDE-SMITH

CONSTABLE & CO. LTD.
LONDON
1924

PRINTED IN GREAT BRITAIN.
CHISWICK PRESS: CHARLES WHITTINGHAM AND GRIGGS (PRINTERS), LTD.
TOOKS COURT, CHANCERY LANE, LONDON.

TO

THE MEMORY

OF

EDGAR FRERE

KILLED IN ACTION

22 MAY 1916

CONTENTS

CONTENTS

CONTENTS

CONTENTS

ACKNOWLEDGEMENTS

MY thanks are due to the kindness of Mrs. Brooke, Mr. Edward Marsh, and Messrs. Sidgwick and Jackson for allowing me to reprint a poem by Rupert Brooke. Mr. Walter de la Mare, Mr. Peter Quennell, Mr. Siegfried Sassoon, Miss Eleanor Farjeon, and my brother, Mr. Graham Royde-Smith, have also most generously given me poems, some of which have not appeared before in any published volume.

I have, further, to thank Mr. Frank Sidgwick for help in verifying certain texts, and also for permission to reprint three carols from *Early English Lyrics*, as well as for his own ballad of Christmas.

Permission to use copyright poems has been obtained from Messrs. Selwyn and Blount for a poem by Edward Thomas; from Mr. Basil Blackwell for a poem by the Rev. A. S. Cripps; from Messrs. Elkin Matthews for poems by Mary Coleridge and by Lionel Johnson; from Messrs. J. M. Dent for a poem by Mr. G. K. Chesterton; from Mr. Jonathan Cape for a poem by Mr. W. H. Davies; from Mr. John Murray for a poem by Dr. Bridges; from Messrs. Macmillan for poems by "A.E.", by T. E. Brown, by Mr. Thomas Hardy, by Mr. Rudyard Kipling, and by Mr. W. B. Yeats; from Messrs. Burns and Oates for two poems by Father Tabb; from Messrs. Duckworth for two poems by Mr. Hilaire Belloc, and from Mr. Martin Secker for *A Fragment* by James Elroy Flecker.

Should the authors of the two anonymous poems included in the following pages ever find their property here, I beg them to accept my thanks, acknowledgements, and apologies for the freedom their modesty has forced upon me.

N.G.R.-S.

AN APOLOGY

THIS collection has no claim to be an anthology of the best, nor even of very good, poems, though some quite bad ones have been taken out of it one by one as it was fashioned. Nor is it a selection of poems in one mood or on one theme. But it has a unity of its own.

It is said that a man's character can be better judged by reading the letters written to him than by reading those he himself has written. If only the same were true of the poems he has loved the best I could, in re-reading this little book, put back all the volumes from which it has been sifted, in a spirit of high and peaceful vanity. But, alas ! the best persons so often have the worst taste, and Good Taste can be the one virtue dwelling in a soul possessed by quite four if not five of the Seven Deadly Sins. So I will make neither excuse nor defence for adding another page to the library of the world's anthologies, but will instead offer an explanation about this one.

Poetry, and more especially lyric poetry, depends for its existence quite as much on the minds which receive as on the poet who sends forth the verse. Indeed, until a poem has made its effect on the ear and the imagination of someone other than the poet who has written it, it cannot exist in any real sense at all. This effect on the recipient is not in any way the test of the poem's worth (some good people are wonderfully moved by quite bad poetry), it merely establishes the poem's existence in a world wherein the bad will perish eventually of its own poor accord. But, true poetry being immortal, the true poem is born again each time it recreates itself in each new lover's mind, and each rebirth is as real an experience for the mind in which it takes place as was the actual conception and creation of the poem to its originator ; is too, in a sense, an invigoration of that poem's identity and worth.

The poet delivers himself of his lyric, and goes on to fresh travail. The poem, a foundling for whom its parent can do no more, must live thereafter on the finder. And there is no adventure so compact of pure delight as this of the finding of poetry. The making, like all creative activity, is a matter of groaning in frustration, and of effort to attain an ideal always unreached even by the most consummate artist in the moment of his finest achievement. But, finding, discovery is all joy and wonder. And it is always sudden, a miracle of chance, a revelation that comes unsought, and only once to an unprepared spirit—but always, like the inspiration visiting the poet in his season only—suddenly and with an illumination as uncontrollable as that of the sun between tracts of cloud.

And, just as if going out to sweep the snow from a winter doorstep you should find a swaddled child ; or, if when digging to break dull ground for cabbages you came upon buried gold, so when some perfunctory reading suddenly brings you to the poem you can make alive, the first sign of recognition is an overwhelming emotion. Later—as it would be if you undertook to adopt the foundling or to bank the treasure—the judgement awakes, tests are made and by them the validity of the experience is proved. Sometimes the emotion, subsiding, leaves no treasure behind. But if the foundling is of the blood royal, if it is not pinchbeck but ingots you have unearthed, the process of vivification continues and the poem itself grows stronger the more you scan it. It is of no importance that other people may not feel the same emotion as you do over the same cause, though it is of the greatest importance that they should, if they are people of any importance at all, give intellectual assent to your declaration that for you this poem is alive. Sometimes indeed, so delicate is the miracle, a fortuitous opinion from outside will crush the life from some new-found and still secret treasure. But this will only happen at the beginning of the adventure. As the hoard increases courage rises : you are ready to defend your foundlings against the very Gosse himself.

These general principles are laid down in no didactic spirit but as a statement of a general truth which seems to me to arise from a personal experience. I have of late begun to examine into the nature and quality of the poems I hold most dear, and in them I find a unity, not of form, but of content, the more remarkable because the poems have not been collected by me but have each in its time taken possession of me, and almost always as I have already said, by surprise. This unity I see to be in a measure my own work.

And here I must become for a page or so unashamed, and go back to the first beginnings of this anthology by way of some early autobiography.

* * * *

I learned to read, very suddenly and rather late in

life, a fortnight after my seventh birthday. Up till this event I had been taught, orally, poetry and the multiplication table, and felt for both an equal if languid hatred. *The Pied Piper of Hamelin*, Blake's *Songs of Innocence*, *The Quality of Mercy*, the 23rd Psalm, and "Eight times eight are"—whatever you say they are, for I can never be immediately certain about the sum—were then, and still remain, matters which leave me a little bored. But having, for purposes of my own, acquired the art of reading between one sunset and another I went, or to be exact, was taken as usual, to public worship on the following Sunday and met Poetry for myself and for the first time with no administrating elder to stand between me and the shock. I told no one at the time, I do not propose even now to tell what verse it was that took form on the pages of the hymn book I was reading and set up in me those strange thrills and shudders which ended in tears and an ignominious hustling out of church into the open air. And that particular verse is not in this book. But the experience was repeated a few days later when I came upon the *Coronach*, and has announced, less violently but quite as surely, each one of the other poems which do find a place here. For the first and most stringent condition I have laid on myself in making this anthology is that it shall consist only of such poems as have taken me by surprise and storm. *No* poem of which I have been warned beforehand, however gladly I have come to recognize it after an introduction, has been admitted. Most of these conquering lyrics have endured the tests of familiarity and discussion. One or two have survived criticism in the strength of that first meeting, the memory of which does not fade. There have been, of course, many poems which began by possessing the mind (or is it the heart?) and ended by leaving nothing but an astonished shame behind them when they were cast out, long before the idea of this anthology began to dawn in my mind.

There are also great poems which had their moment in spite of all that Authority could do in the matter of dragooning admiration to death. *Lycidas* is one of them. I grew up hating Milton. "Organ-voiced" is still to me an occasion for that particular disgusted shrug only known to members of large families who have learned a conspiratorial gesture to express deep and necessarily secret contempt for the enthusiasms of the elderly. In the inexorable condemnations of an enlightened nursery the phrase "that two-handed engine at the door" went into the same class as the unwieldy elephant wreathing his lithe proboscis. Milton clearly was one of those creatures, generally masculine, who showed off—an obliterating offence.

But one July afternoon, in the days when Milton was still a bore, there was a school concert. Looking out through an open window into the garden where I might have been walking with a friend instead of listening to the simpler works of Bach, Chopin, and Schumann executed with that clear absence of any feeling save nervousness, peculiar to school concerts, I fell into one of those golden reveries which are the glory of adolescence. Into that dream there broke the voice of a younger sister, a creature who till that moment had displayed all but the nobler characteristics of unruly childhood, and who, in face of the appalling nature of her piano-work had been degraded to the rank of those who recite. Why she had chosen *Lycidas* I cannot say. She was at that time far more likely to have said *John Gilpin* or the *Absent-Minded Beggar*, a poem much in favour that year. She may possibly have done it to annoy. *Lycidas* is a long, long poem, and she was an ingeniously annoying child. But for some reason or other the voice I knew so well as a conveyer of ribaldry and defiance was now saying:

> Together both, ere the high lawns appeared
> Under the opening eyelids of the morn
> We drove afield. . . .

And it was a soft and beautiful voice, and the mind that controlled it was telling the sumptuous verses with feeling, with an intelligence, and a sense of beauty so alien to the manifestations of its private life, that I knew for the first time that my very trying relative had a soul. And so *Lycidas* and my young sister became real together, and Milton was forgiven and exalted.

But *Lycidas* is more than a lyric, and for other reasons it is not in this book, though if it were it would have to go with *Adonais*, a poem which has probably been the arouser of a sense of poetry in more people than any other written since its day. Also, I have, with an exception here and there (all of these will be patent to the reader), kept away from the great anthologies in making this one.

The most notable of these exceptions is the poem I have set apart on the page which follows this preface.

The history of its existence in my world illustrates the principle I have discovered to underlie the whole selection. I must have known the poem long before I noticed it. But one day some one in conversation said:

The eclipse and glory of her kind.

This was so clearly a quotation that I sought out the speaker at a convenient season and demanded its origin. Being told to look in *The Golden Treasury*, I was rewarded by the discovery of the five-line stanza, a beauty always apparent even when it is used by an unworthy pen. For some days I nursed the revelation, turning the magic of that extra line over in my enchanted mind, until, suddenly, a glory within the glory already apprehended, the floating *O's* of the second stanza bloomed on my ear (almost on my tongue) like an ineffable savour, ambrosial, increasing as it was re-tasted. And from the Rose I turned back to the Moon and found the sob of joy, which the first question raised as I said it aloud to my listening self, break into a giggle at the deriding ease of

You common people of the skies.

So often as I came back to this miracle, so often I found it renewed. Later on, when I knew with my mind as well as with my ear and heart, I learnt to praise its structure, and to admire the consummate naturalness of its artificiality, and I now hold it to be the most perfect of all English lyrics, unrivalled for sheer sustained flawlessness by any poet until certain living writers began to make Georgian lyrics. And of their songs nobody can prophesy with authority until they are seen down the perspective of the years after their authors' days are ended.

Such, then, in varying degree, has been my experience with all the poems here collected, though very few of them have yielded so unfailing a renewal of discovery as Sir Thomas Wotton's, which is why Elizabeth of Bohemia is here once again set apart from all other beauties in a place alone.

Strangely and perhaps not very creditably one or two of the modern poems which have been acclaimed by popular or by educated taste, after I had found them myself, have lost their savour in my mind, and there are some poems (*Innisfree* and *Arabia* are among them) about which I feel as I felt about the multiplication table; faultless in themselves they are the occasion of airs in others and draw no love from me.

This therefore is a wilful and prejudiced book so far as its exclusions go. Many of the poems I have left out of it are as the bread (though not the breath) of life to me. But they are to be found in most of the other anthologies. So far as the inclusions go they are all of the desert island class. I would not be shipwrecked without any one of them. None of them is an entirely bad poem, but some not entirely perfect poems are here because of such bursts of splendour as

> Hearing oblivion beyond memory

or

> Thy grave! To which my thoughts shall move
> Like bees in storm into their hive.

There are cases in which the lovely moment does not quite outweigh some failure in my response to its content. One of them is Alice Meynell's sonnet *My Garden* with its lovely singing close:

For as these come and go and quit our pine
To follow the sweet season, or, new comers
Sing one song only from our alder trees
My heart has thoughts, which though thine eyes hold mine,
Flit to the silent world and other summers. . . .

I can never be sure when these lines will not come rippling back along the waves of memory to fill an empty breath with delight—but I cannot even remember the rest of this poem, and that is why I have not asked to be allowed to put it in my book.

And there are some poems, like the one which first carried me into the adventure of poetry-seeking, which I would not put into any printed book because there are moments no one can be expected to share with other men. Christina Rossetti, except for *Sleep at Sea*, belongs to this division of experience. To tell about her triumphs in the heart must be for everybody more of a personal confession than a literary judgment. It is the same with *A Shropshire Lad*. Even if they were available for an anthology, the poems in that sequence which belong to my own adventure belong to that part of it which is not for publication, though I would, if I might, put here the whole of the loveliest lyric in *Last Poems*, the one which begins:

Tell me not here, it needs not saying
What tune the Enchantress plays
In aftermaths of soft Septembers
Or under blanching mays,
For she and I were long acquainted
And I know all her ways. . . .

With one exception I have quoted the whole of

every poem in which any transporting passage may be hidden, holding the chopping ways of some anthologists a grave discourtesy, as though we should refuse to listen to a guest except when he speaks in epigrams.

So with all its reserves and rejections, this book is a record of experience made in the belief that, read as a whole, it may convey with a beauty and a force for ever beyond my power of expression some sense of the unpremeditated and inexhaustible adventure out of which it has arisen.

SIR HENRY WOTTON

TO

ELIZABETH OF BOHEMIA

YOU meaner beauties of the night,
   That poorly satisfy our eyes
More by your number than your light,
   You common people of the skies,
What are you, when the Moon shall rise?

Ye violets that first appear,
   By your pure purple mantles known
Like the proud virgins of the year,
   As if the spring were all your own,—
What are you when the Rose is blown?

Ye curious chanters of the wood
   That warble forth dame Nature's lays,
Thinking your passions understood
   By your weak accents; what 's your praise
When Philomel her voice doth raise?

So when my Mistress shall be seen
   In sweetness of her looks and mind,
By virtue first, then choice, a Queen,
   Tell me, if she were not design'd
Th' eclipse and glory of her kind?

BIRDS AND TREES

I HAVE a gentil cok
Croweth me day;
He doth me risen erly
My matines for to say.

I have a gentil cok;
Comen he is of grete;
His comb is of red corel,
His tail is of get.

I have a gentil cok;
Comen he is of kinde;
His comb is of red corel,
His tail is of inde.

His leggés ben of asour,
So gentil and so smale;
His sporés arn of silver white
Into the wortéwale.*

His eynen arn of cristal,
Loken all in aumber;
And every night he percheth him
In mine ladyes chaumber.

Carol from the Sloane MS.

* The skin of the claws.

A FRANCISCAN PRAYER

WHEN we are past
Woodlands and moonshine nights—
Consume them not nor in the dust-wrack cast!
Save them for bat and owl,
And all night beasts that prowl,
And for night-warbling birds therein to sing
All an eternal spring;

When we are past
Fresh uplands, flaming dawns—
Consume them not nor in the dust-wrack cast!
Save them for horse and hound,
Elm rooks and lark a-ground,
And for the proud red cocks therein to crow
The East's abiding glow!

When we are past
Bare veld and breadth of sky—
Consume them not nor in the dust-wrack cast!
Save them for all shy things
Fleet-footed, wild of wings—
To hold thanksgiving there, as well they may,
That we are gone for aye!

ARTHUR SHIRLEY CRIPPS.

PROCNE

(A FRAGMENT)

SO she became a bird and bird-like danced
On a long sloe-bough, treading the silver blossom
With a bird's lovely feet,
And shaken blossoms fell into the hands
Of Sunlight. And he held them for a moment
And let them drop.
And in the autumn Procne came again
And leapt upon the crooked sloe-bough singing,
And the dark berries winked like earth-dimmed beads,
As the branch swung beneath her dancing feet.

P. C. QUENNELL.

THE TIMBER

SURE thou didst flourish once! and many springs,
  Many bright mornings, much dew, many showers
Past o'er thy head: many light hearts and wings,
  Which now are dead, lodg'd in thy living bowers.

And still a new succession sings and flies;
  Fresh groves grow up, and their green branches shoot
Towards the old and still enduring skies;
  While the low violet thrives at their root.

But thou beneath the sad and heavy line
  Of death doth waste all senseless, cold, and dark;
Where not so much as dreams of light may shine,
  Nor any thought of greenness, leaf, or bark.

And yet, as if some deep hate, and dissent,
  Bred in thy growth betwixt high winds and thee,
Were still alive, thou dost great storms resent,
  Before they come, and know'st how near they be.

Else all at rest thou lyest, and the fierce breath
  Of tempests can no more disturb thy ease;
But this thy strange resentment after death
  Means onely those who broke in life thy peace.

So murthered man, when lovely life is done,
  And his blood freez'd, keeps in the center still
Some secret sense, which makes the dead blood run
  At his approach that did the body kill.

And is there any murth'rer worse than sin?
  Or any storms more foul than a lewd life?
Or what resentient can work more within,
  Than true remorse, when with past sins at strife?

He that hath left life's vain joys and vain care,
  And truly hates to be detain'd on earth
Hath got a house where many mansions are,
  And keeps his soul unto eternal mirth.

But though thus dead unto the world, and ceas'd
  From sin, he walks a narrow, private way;
Yet grief and old wounds make him sore displeas'd,
  And all his life a rainy, weeping day.

For though he should forsake the world, and live
  As meer a stranger, as men long since dead;
Yet joy itself will make a right soul grieve
  To think, he should be so long vainly led.

But as shades set off light, so tears and grief,
  Though of themselves but a sad blubber'd story,
By shewing the sin great, shew the relief
  Far greater, and so speak my Saviour's glory.

If my way lies through deserts and wilde woods,
  Where all the land with scorching heat is curst;
Better the pools should flow with rain and floods
  To fill my bottle when I die with thirst.

Blest showers they are, and streams sent from above;
  Begetting virgins where they use to flow;
The trees of life no other waters love,
  These upper springs, and none else make them grow.

But these chaste fountains flow not till we dye.
  Some drops may fall before; but a clear spring
And ever running, till we leave to fling
  Dirt in her way, will keep above the sky.

HENRY VAUGHAN.

A BALLAD OF TREES AND THE MASTER

INTO the woods my Master went,
  Clean forspent, forspent,
Into the woods my Master came
Forspent with love and shame.
But the olives they were not blind to Him,
And the little grey leaves were kind to Him,
The thorn-tree had a mind to Him
When into the woods He came.

Out of the woods my Master went,
And He was well content.
Out of the woods my Master came
Content with Death and Shame.
When Death and Shame would woo Him last
From under the trees they drew Him last,
'Twas on a tree they slew Him—last
When out of the woods He came.

SYDNEY LANIER.

BIRD AND BROOK

MY song, that 's bird-like in its kind,
  Is in the mind,
Love—in the mind;
And in my season I am moved
No more or less from being loved;
No woman's love has power to bring
My song back when I cease to sing;
Nor can she, when my season 's strong,
Prevent my mind from song.

But where I feel your woman's part,
Is in the heart,
Love—in the heart;
For when that bird of mine broods long,
And I'd be sad without my song,
Your love then makes my heart a brook
That dreams in many a quiet nook,
And makes a steady, murmuring sound
Of joy the whole year round.

WILLIAM H. DAVIES.

NIGHT AND DAY

SONNET

WHEN I recall Time's tedious overthrow,
  The pride of seasons that must stoop to change,
How no availing auguries foreshow
  Ere night be near that shall our days estrange.

When I remember how resplendent June
  Last year made mockery of the proud pied spring,
How the sure amber-eyed autumnal moon
  Saw June unparadised, no choir to sing;

That all the riches of earth's sights and sounds
  Are but base coinage of the merchant sense,
How Life flies low upon a little ground
  And yet outlasts its poor magnificence;

O Love! I dare not set a love of ours
Above the passage of the imperious hours.

Pall Mall Gazette, Jan. 1896.

DAYS

DAMSELS of Time, the hypocritic Days,
Muffled and dumb like barefoot dervishes,
And marching single in an endless file,
Bring diadems and faggots in their hands.
To each they offer gifts after his will,
Bread, kingdoms, stars, and sky that holds them all.
I, in my pleachéd garden, watched the pomp,
Forgot my morning wishes, hastily
Took a few herbs and apples, and the Day
Turned and departed silent. I, too late,
Under her solemn fillet saw the scorn.

RALPH WALDO EMERSON.

FOLLOW thy fair sun, unhappy shadow!
Though thou be black as night,
And she made all of light,
Yet follow thy fair sun, unhappy shadow!

Follow her whose light thy light depriveth;
Though here thou livest disgraced,
And she in heaven is placed,
Yet follow her whose light the world reviveth!

Follow those pure beams whose beauty burneth,
That so have scorched thee,
As thou still black must be,
Till her kind beams thy black to brightness turneth.

Follow her! while yet her glory shineth:
There comes a luckless night,
That will dim all her light;
And this the black unhappy shade divineth.

Follow still! since so thy fates ordained;
The sun must have his shade,
Till both at once do fade;
The sun still proved, the shadow still disdained.

THOMAS CAMPION.

THE MOON'S FUNERAL

THE Moon is dead! I saw her die.
She in a drifting cloud was drest,
She lay along the uncertain west,
A dream to see,
And very low she spake to me:
"I go where none may understand,
I fade into the nameless land,
And there must lie perpetually"—
And therefore loudly, loudly I
And high
And very piteously make cry:
The Moon is dead! I saw her die.

And will she never rise again,
The Holy Moon? Oh, never more!
Perhaps along the inhuman shore
Where pale ghosts are,
Beyond the far Lethean fen
She and some wide infernal star——

To us who loved her never more,
The Moon will never rise again.
Oh! never more in nightly sky
Her eye so high shall peep and pry,
To see the great world rolling by.
For why?
The Moon is dead. I saw her die.

HILAIRE BELLOC.

THE NIGHT WILL NEVER STAY

THE night will never stay,
 The night will still go by,
Though with a million stars
You pin it to the sky;
Though you bind it with the blowing wind
And buckle it with the moon,
The night will slip away
Like sorrow or a tune.

ELEANOR FARJEON.

AT DUSK

LEFT to the stars the sky,
  Left to the sea the sand,
Softly the small waves drop
  Hand on white hand:
Where murmuring hills are steep
Countless musicians keep
  Tryst, among wild, dim valleys
Lost in sleep.

Their music binds a world
  Of alien fields unknown,
Stirs among cloud-hung peaks
  Lovely and lone.
Far and remote they seem,
Playing their endless theme—
  Thin threads of sound come trembling back,
Dream upon dream.

ENID HAMILTON-FELLOWS.

THE WORLD

"CITIES AND THRONES AND POWERS"

CITIES and Thrones and Powers,
Stand in Time's eye,
Almost as long as flowers,
Which daily die:
But, as new buds put forth
To glad new men,
Out of the spent and unconsidered Earth
The Cities rise again.

This Season's Daffodil,
She never hears,
What change, what chance, what chill,
Cut down last year's;
But with bold countenance,
And knowledge small,
Esteems her seven days' continuance
To be perpetual.

So Time, that is o'er kind,
To all that be,
Ordains us e'en as blind,
As bold as she:
That in our very death,
And burial sure,
Shadow to shadow, well persuaded, saith,
"See how our works endure!"

RUDYARD KIPLING.

OZYMANDIAS

I MET a traveller from an antique land
Who said: "Two vast and trunkless legs of stone
Stand in the desert. Near them, on the sand,
Half sunk, a shattered visage lies, whose frown,
And wrinkled lip, and sneer of cold command,
Tell that its sculptor well those passions read
Which yet survive, stamped on these lifeless things,
The hand that mocked them and the heart that fed:
And on the pedestal these words appear:
"My name is Ozymandias, king of kings:
Look on my works, ye Mighty, and despair!"
Nothing beside remains. Round the decay
Of that colossal wreck, boundless and bare
The lone and level sands stretch far away.

SHELLEY.

GONE IN THE WIND

SOLOMON, where is thy throne? It is gone in the wind.
Babylon, where is thy might? It is gone in the wind.
Like the swift shadows of noon, like the dreams of the blind,
Vanish the glories and pomps of the earth in the wind.

Man, canst thou build upon aught in the pride of thy mind?
Wisdom will teach thee that nothing can tarry behind:
Tho' there be thousand bright actions embalm'd and enshrined,
Myriads and millions of brighter are snow in the wind.

Solomon, where is thy throne? It is gone in the wind.
Babylon, where is thy might? It is gone in the wind.
All that the genius of man hath achieved or design'd
Waits but its hour to be dealt with as dust by the wind.

Say what is pleasure? A phantom, a mask undefined:
Science? An almond whereof we can pierce but the rind:
Honour and affluence? Firmans that Fortune has sign'd,
Only to glitter and pass on the wings of the wind.

Solomon, where is thy throne? It is gone in the wind.
Babylon, where is thy might? It is gone in the wind.
Who is the fortunate? *He who in anguish hath pined!*
He shall rejoice when his relics are dust in the wind.

Mortal, be careful with what thy best hopes are entwined:
Woe to the miners for Truth, where the lampless have mined!
Woe to the seekers on earth for what none ever find!
They and their trust shall be scatter'd like leaves to the wind!

Solomon, where is thy throne? It is gone in the wind.
Babylon, where is thy might? It is gone in the wind.
Happy in death are they only whose hearts have consign'd
All earth's affections and longings and cares to the wind.

Pity thou reader, the madness of poor humankind
Raving of knowledge—and Satan so busy to blind!
Raving of glory, like me; for the garlands I bind,
Garlands of song, are but gather'd—and strewn in the wind.

Solomon, where is thy throne? It is gone in the wind.
Babylon, where is thy might? It is gone in the wind.
I, Abul-Namez, must rest; for my fire is declined,
And I hear voices from Hades like bells on the wind.

JAMES CLARENCE MANGAN.

THE END

AFTER the blast of lightening from the east,
  The flourish of loud clouds; the Chariot Throne,
After the drums of time have rolled and ceased,
  And from the bronze west, long retreat is blown,

Shall Life renew these bodies? Of a truth
  All death will he annul, all tears assuage?
Or fill these void veins full again with youth,
  And wash, with an immortal water, age?

When I do ask white Age, he saith, "Not so.
  My head hangs weighed with snow."
And when I hearken to the Earth, she saith:
  "My fiery heart shrinks, aching. It is death.
My ancient scars shall not be glorified,
Nor my titanic tears, the seas, be dried."

WILFRED OWEN.
(*Killed in action*, 4 *November* 1918.)

WHEN THE WORLD IS BURNING

WHEN the world is burning,
Fired within, yet turning
Round with face unscathed,—
Ere fierce flames, uprushing,
O'er all lands leap, crushing,
Till earth fall, fire-swathed;
Up amidst the meadows,
Gently through the shadows,
Gentle flames will glide,
Small and blue and golden:
Though by bard beholden
When in calm dreams folden,
Calm his dreams will bide.

When the dance is sweeping,
Through the greensward peeping
Shall the soft lights start;
Laughing maids, unstaying,
Deeming it trick-playing,
High their robes upswaying,
O'er the lights shall dart;
And the woodland haunter
Shall not cease to saunter
When, far down some glade,
Of the great world's burning,
One soft flame upturning,
Seems, to his discerning,
Crocus in the shade.

EBENEZER JONES.

THE UNKNOWN

SUDDEN LIGHT

I HAVE been here before,
But when or how I cannot tell:
I know the grass beyond the door,
The sweet keen smell,
The sighing sound, the lights around the shore.

You have been mine before,—
How long ago I may not know:
But just when at that swallow's soar
Your neck turned so,
Some veil did fall,—I knew it all of yore.

Has this been thus before?
And shall not thus time's eddying flight
Still with our lives our love restore
In death's despite,
And day and night yield one delight once more?

D. G. Rossetti.

THE CLOUD CONFINES

THE day is dark and the night
To him that would search their heart,
No lips of cloud that will part
Nor morning song in the light:
Only, gazing alone,
To him wild shadows are shown,
Deep under deep unknown
And height above unknown height.
Still we say as we go,—
"Strange to think by the way,
Whatever there is to know,
That shall we know one day."

The Past is over and fled;
Named new, we name it the old;
Thereof some tale hath been told,
But no word comes from the dead;
Whether at all they be,
Or whether as bond or free,
Or whether they too were we,
Or by what spell they have sped.
Still we say as we go,—
"Strange to think by the way,
Whatever there is to know,
That shall we know one day."

What of the heart of hate
That beats in thy breast, O Time?—
Red strife from the furthest prime,
And anguish of fierce debate;
War that shatters her slain,
And peace that grinds them as grain,
And eyes fixed ever in vain
On the pitiless eyes of Fate.

Still we say as we go,—
"Strange to think by the way,
Whatever there is to know,
That shall we know one day."

What of the heart of love
That bleeds in thy breast, O Man?—
Thy kisses snatched 'neath the ban
Of fangs that mock them above;
Thy bells prolonged unto knells,
Thy hope that a breath dispels,
Thy bitter forlorn farewells
And the empty echoes thereof?
Still we say as we go,—
"Strange to think by the way,
Whatever there is to know,
That shall we know one day."

The sky leans dumb on the sea,
Aweary with all its wings;
And oh! the song the sea sings
Is dark everlastingly.
Our past is clean forgot,
Our present is and is not,
Our future 's a sealed seedplot,
And what betwixt them are we?—
We who say as we go,—
"Strange to think by the way,
Whatever there is to know,
That shall we know one day."

D. G. Rossetti.

HYMN TO GOD, MY GOD, IN MY SICKNESS

SINCE I am coming to that Holy room,
  Where, with Thy choir of saints for evermore,
I shall be made Thy music; as I come
  I tune the instrument here at the door,
  And what I must do then, think here before;

Whilst my physicians by their love are grown
  Cosmographers, and I their map, who lie
Flat on this bed, that by them may be shown
  That this is my south-west discovery,
  Per fretum febris, by these straits to die;

I joy, that in these straits I see my west;
  For, though these currents yield return to none,
What shall my west hurt me? As west and east
  In all flat maps—and I am one—are one,
  So death doth touch the resurrection.

Is the Pacific sea my home? Or are
  The eastern riches? Is Jerusalem?
Anyan, and Magellan, and Gibraltar?
  All straits, and none but straits, are ways to them
  Whether where Japhet dwelt, or Cham, or Shem.

We think that Paradise and Calvary,
  Christ's cross and Adam's tree, stood in one place;
Look, Lord, and find both Adams meet in me;
  As the first Adam's sweat surrounds my face,
  May the last Adam's blood my soul embrace.

So, in His purple wrapp'd, receive me, Lord;
  By these His thorns, give me His other crown;
And as to others' souls I preach'd Thy word,
  Be this my text, my sermon to mine own,
  "Therefore that He may raise, the Lord throws
      down."

JOHN DONNE.

THE WHITE ISLAND

IN this world (the Isle of Dreames)
While we sit by sorrowes streames,
Tears and terrors are our theames
Reciting:

But when once from hence we flie,
More and more approaching nigh
Unto young Eternitie
Uniting:

In that whiter Island, where
Things are evermore sincere;
Candor here, and lustre there
Delighting:

There no monstrous fancies shall
Out of hell an horrour call,
To create (or cause at all)
Affrighting.

There in calm and cooling sleep
We our eyes shall never steep;
But eternall watch shall keep,
Attending.

Pleasures, such as shall pursue
Me immortaliz'd, and you;
And fresh joyes, as never to
Have ending.

ROBERT HERRICK.

PEACE

MY Soul, there is a countrie
   Afar beyond the stars,
Where stands a winged Sentrie
   All skilfull in the wars.
There, above noise and danger,
   Sweet peace sits, crowned with smiles,
And One born in a manger
   Commands the beauteous files.
He is thy gracious friend
   And (O my Soul awake!)
Did in pure love descend,
   To die here for thy sake.
If thou canst get but thither,
   There grows the flowre of peace,
The rose that cannot wither,
   Thy fortress, and thy ease.
Leave then thy foolish ranges;
   For none can thee secure,
But One, who never changes,
   Thy God, thy Life, thy Cure.

HENRY VAUGHAN.

I DREAM'D there would be spring no more,
  That nature's ancient power was lost:
  The streets were black with smoke and frost,
They chatter'd trifles at the door:

I wander'd from the noisy town,
  I found a wood with thorny boughs:
  I took the thorns to bind my brows,
I wore them like a civic crown:

I met with scoffs, I met with scorns
  From youth and babe and hoary hairs:
  They call'd me in the public squares
The fool that wears a crown of thorns!

They call'd me fool, they call'd me child:
  I found an angel of the night;
  The voice was low, the look was bright;
He look'd upon my crown and smiled:

He reach'd the glory of a hand,
  That seem'd to touch it into leaf:
  The voice was not the voice of grief,
The words were hard to understand.

TENNYSON.
From *In Memoriam*.

THE MONOCHORD

IS it this sky's vast vault or ocean's sound
That is Life's self and draws my life from me,
And by instinct, ineffable decree
Holds my breath quailing on the bitter bound?
Nay, is it Life or Death, thus thunder-crowned,
That 'mid the tide of all emergency
Now notes my separate wave, and to what sea
Its difficult eddies labour in the ground?

Oh! what is this that knows the road I came,
The flame turned cloud, the cloud returned to flame,
The lifted shifted steeps and all the way,
That draws round me at last this wind-warm space,
And in regenerate rapture turns my face
Upon the devious coverts of dismay?

D. G. Rossetti.

HER FAITH

BECAUSE my faltering feet will fail to dare
The downward of the endless steps of Hell,
Give me the word in Time that triumphs there.
I too must go into the dreadful Hollow,
Where all our human laughter stops—and hark!
The tiny, stuffless voices of the dark
Have called me, called me till I needs must follow.
Give me the word and I'll attempt it well.

Say it 's the little winking of an eye,
Which in that issue is uncurtained quite,
A little sleep that helps a moment by
Between the thin dawn and the bare daylight.
Oh! tell me more than yet was hoped of men,
Swear that 's true now, and I'll believe it then.

HILAIRE BELLOC.

LIFE

TO TIRZAH

WHATE'ER is born of mortal birth
Must be consumèd with the earth,
To rise from generation free :
Then what have I to do with thee ?

The sexes sprung from shame and pride,
Blowed in the morn, in evening died,
But mercy changed death into sleep ;
The sexes rose to work and weep.

Thou, mother of my mortal part,
With cruelty didst mould my heart,
And with false self-deceiving tears
Didst blind my nostrils, eyes and ears,

Didst close my tongue in senseless clay,
And me to mortal life betray.
The death of Jesus set me free :
Then what have I to do with thee ?

WILLIAM BLAKE.

THE AFFLICTION OF RICHARD

LOVE not too much. But how,
  When thou hast made me such,
And dost my gifts bestow,
  How can I love too much ?
Though I must fear to lose,
  And drown my joy in care,
With all its thorns I choose
  The path of love and prayer.

Though thou, I know not why,
  Didst kill my childish trust,
That breach with toil did I
  Repair, because I must :
And spite of frightening schemes,
  Which with the fiends of Hell
Blaspheme thee in my dreams,
  So far I have hoped well.

But what the heavenly key,
  What marvel in me wrought
Shall quite exculpate thee,
  I have no shadow of thought,
What am I that complain ?
  My love, from which began
My question sad and vain,
  Justifies thee to man.

ROBERT BRIDGES.

SHADOW

CHILD of my love! though thou be bright as day,
Though all the sons of joy laugh and adore thee,
Thou canst not throw thy shadow self away.
Where thou dost come, the earth is darker for thee.

When thou dost pass, a flower that saw the sun
Sees him no longer.
The hosts of darkness are, thou radiant one,
Through thee made stronger!

MARY E. COLERIDGE.

LIFE

ME, in the midst of dateless centuries,
By Love concealed,
Now, newly swathed in mortal destinies,
Hath Time revealed.

A breathing space, a silence, and behold
What I have been,
Unswathed, the circling centuries enfold,
Again unseen.

With Days and Nights brief fellowship was mine;
But unto thee
I come, a child inseparably thine,
Eternity.

JOHN BANNISTER TABB.

THE DARK ANGEL

DARK Angel, with thine aching lust
  To rid the world of penitence:
Malicious Angel, who still dost
  My soul such subtile violence!

Because of thee, no thought, no thing,
  Abides for me undesecrate:
Dark Angel, ever on the wing,
  Who never reachest me too late!

When music sounds, then changest thou
  Its silvery to a sultry fire:
Nor will thine envious heart allow
  Delight untortured by desire.

Through thee, the gracious Muses turn
  To Furies, O mine Enemy!
And all the things of beauty burn
  With flames of evil ecstacy.

Because of thee, the land of dreams
  Becomes a gathering place of fears:
Until tormented slumber seems
  One vehemence of useless tears.

When sunlight glows upon the flowers,
  Or ripples down the dancing sea:
Thou with thy troop of passionate powers,
  Beleaguerest, bewilderest, me.

Within the breath of autumn woods,
  Within the winter silences:
Thy venomous spirit stirs and broods,
  O Master of impieties!

The ardour of red flame is thine,
  And thine the steely soul of ice:
Thou poisonest the fair design
  Of nature, with unfair device.

Apples of ashes, golden bright;
  Waters of bitterness, how sweet!
O banquet of a foul delight,
  Prepared by thee, dark Paraclete!

Thou art the whisper in the gloom,
  The hinting tone, the haunting laugh:
Thou art the adorner of my tomb,
  The minstrel of mine epitaph.

I fight thee, in the Holy Name!
  Yet, what thou dost, is what God saith:
Tempter! should I escape thy flame,
  Thou wilt have helped my soul from Death:

The second Death, that never dies,
  That cannot die, when time is dead:
Live Death, wherein the lost soul cries,
  Eternally uncomforted.

Dark Angel, with thine aching lust!
  Of two defeats, of two despairs:
Less dread, a change to drifting dust,
  Than thine eternity of cares.

Do what thou wilt, thou shalt not so,
  Dark Angel! triumph over me:
Lonely unto the Lone I go:
  Divine to the Divinity.

LIONEL JOHNSON.

THE VICTORS

WE came not in with proud
    Firm martial footsteps in a measured tread
Slow pacing to the crash of music loud,
  No gorgeous trophies went before, no crowd
Of captives followed us with drooping head,
  No shining laurel sceptred us, nor crowned,
Nor with its leaf our glittering lances bound.
  "This looks not like a Triumph" then they said.
With faces darkened in the battle flame,
  With banners faded from their early pride,
Through wind and sun and showers of bleaching rain,
  Yet red in all our garments deeply dyed,
With many a wound upon us, many a stain,
  We came with steps that faltered—yet we came.

ANON.

THE QUEEN'S MEN

VALOUR and Innocence
Have latterly gone hence
To certain death by certain shame attended.
Envy—ah! even to tears!—
The fortune of their years
Which, though so few, yet so divinely ended.

Scarce had they lifted up
Life's full and fiery cup,
Than they had set it down untouched before them.
Before their day arose
They beckoned it to close—
Close in confusion and destruction o'er them.

They did not stay to ask
What prize should crown their task—
Well sure that prize was such as no man strives for;
But passed into eclipse,
Her kiss upon their lips—
Even Belphoebe's, whom they gave their lives for!

RUDYARD KIPLING.

A FRAGMENT

O POURING westering streams
Shouting that I have leapt the mountain bar,
Down curve on curve my journey's white way gleams—
My road along the river of return,

I know the countries where the white moons burn,
And heavy star on star
Dips on the pale and crystal desert hills.
I know the river of the sun that fills
With founts of gold the lakes of Orient sky.

* * * * *

And I have heard a voice of broken seas
And from the cliffs a cry.
Ah still they learn, those cave-eared Cyclades,
The Triton's friendly or his fearful horn
And why the deep sea bells but seldom chime,
And how those waves and with what spell-swept rhyme
In years of morning, on a summer's morn
Whispering round his castle on the coast,
Lured young Achilles from his haunted sleep
And drave him out to dive beyond those deep
Dim purple windows of the empty swell,
His ivory body flitting like a ghost
Over the holes where flat blind fishes dwell,
All to embrace his mother thronèd in her shell.

JAMES ELROY FLECKER.

CELIA'S FALL

CELIA, my fairest Celia, fell,
Celia, than the fairest, fairer,
Celia (with none I must compare her)
That all alone is all in all,
Of what we fair, and modest call,
Celia, white as alabaster,
Celia, than Diana chaster,
This fair, fair Celia, grief to tell,
This fair, this modest, chaste one fell.

My Celia, sweetest Celia fell,
As I have seen a snow-white dove
Decline her bosom from above,
And down her spotless body fling
Without the motion of the wing,
Till she arrest her seeming fall
Upon some happy pedestal:
So soft this sweet, I love so well,
This sweet, this dove-like Celia, fell.

Celia, my dearest Celia fell,
As I have seen a melting star
Drop down its fire from its sphere,
Rescuing so its glorious sight
From that paler snuff of light:
Yet is a star bright and entire,
As when 'twas wrappèd in all that fire:
So bright this dear, I love so well,
This dear, this star-like Celia fell.

And yet my Celia did not fall
As grosser earthly mortals do,
But stoop'd, like Phoebus, to renew
Her lustre by her morning rise,
And dart new beauties in the skies,

Like a white dove, she took her flight,
And like a star, she shot her light;
This dove, this star, so lov'd of all,
My Fair, Dear, Sweetest, did not fall.

But, if you'll say my Celia fell,
Of this I'm sure, that, like the dart
Of Love it was, and on my heart;
Poor heart alas! wounded before,
She needed not have hurt it more:
So absolute a conquest she
Had gainèd before of it, and me,
That neither of us had been well
Before, or since my Celia fell.

CHARLES COTTON.

A SONNET FROM THE PORTUGUESE

ACCUSE me not, beseech thee, that I wear
Too calm and sad a face in front of thine:
For we two look two ways, and cannot shine
With the same sunlight on our brow and hair.
On me thou lookest with no doubting care,
As on a bee shut in a crystalline;
Since sorrow hath shut me safe in love's divine,
And to spread wing and fly in the outer air
Were most impossible failure, if I strove
To fail so. But I look on thee—on thee—
Beholding, besides love, the end of love,
Hearing oblivion beyond memory;
As one who sits and gazes from above,
Over the rivers to the bitter sea.

ELIZABETH BARRETT BROWNING.

LET ME ENJOY

LET me enjoy the earth no less
  Because the all-enacting Might
That fashioned forth its loveliness
  Had other aims than my delight.

About my path there flits a fair,
  Who throws me not a word or sign;
I'll charm me with her ignoring air,
  And laud the lips not meant for mine.

From manuscripts of moving song
  Inspired by scenes and souls unknown,
I'll pour out raptures that belong
  To others, as they were my own.

And some day hence, toward Paradise
  And all its blest—if such should be—
I will lift glad, afar-off eyes,
  Though it contain no place for me.

THOMAS HARDY.

LOVE AND DEATH

BALLADE FOR A BIRTHDAY

TIME is our foe.
  After another year
(Ah! breathe it low),
  If you and I are here,
Though you begin to fear
  I may forget I swore
Always to love you, Dear.
  I shall but love you more.

The rose may blow,
  And Autumn chill and drear
Dull the young glow
  Of your sweet face. A tear
May fall if you should hear
  My love, like men's before,
Will pass into the sere.
  I shall but love you more.

The years will go,
  And you, without a peer,
Will older grow,
  And, growing, grow more near
To me. The Wits will sneer,
  And worldly wise three score
Opine that I grow queer.
  I shall but love you more.

Child! Let them jeer—
  The wise, so full of lore,
Be of good cheer.
  I shall but love you more.

GRAHAM ROYDE-SMITH.

SO sweet is thy discourse to me,
  And so delightful is thy sight,
As I taste nothing right but thee:
  O why invented Nature light
Was it alone for Beauty's sake
That her graced words might better take?

No more can I old joys recall,
  They now to me become unknown,
Not seeming to have been at all:
  Alas, how soon is this love grown
To such a spreading height in me
As with it all must shadowed be!

From CAMPION'S *Fourth Book of Airs.*

THE MASK

"PUT off that mask of burning gold
With emerald eyes."
"O no, my dear, you make so bold
To find if hearts be wild and wise,
And yet not cold."

"I would but find what 's there to find,
Love or deceit."
"It was the mask engaged your mind,
And after set your heart to beat,
Not what 's behind."

"But lest you are my enemy,
I must enquire."
"O no, my dear, let all that be,
What matter, so there is but fire
In you, in me?"

WILLIAM BUTLER YEATS.

AGAINST UNWORTHY PRAISE

O HEART, be at peace, because
Nor knave nor dolt can break
What 's not for their applause,
Being for a woman's sake.
Enough if the work has seemed,
So did she your strength renew,
A dream that a lion had dreamed
Till the wilderness cried aloud,
A secret between you two,
Between the proud and the proud.

What, still you would have their praise!
But here 's a haughtier text,
The labyrinth of her days
That her own strangeness perplexed;
And how what her dreaming gave
Earned slander, ingratitude,
From self-same dolt and knave;
Aye, and worse wrong than these.
Yet she, singing upon her road,
Half lion, half child, is at peace.

WILLIAM BUTLER YEATS.

HEARTSEASE

NO more the days
  Are potent to divide
Heart of my heart, my soul's desire from me;
  From dawn to eventide
Our feet have ceased from following lonely ways
  In streets, or by grey margent of the sea.

Even in sleep
  We know each other near,
Old evil dreams to vex us strive in vain,
  The worst of fancied fear—
Of yearning severance—wakes us but to creep
  Into each other's arms to sleep again.

And the kind night
  Steps softly down—
The envious night that always came too soon—
  Now royally to crown
The jocund morn, the smiling afternoon
  With Love's unspeakable, unmatched delight.

ANON.

THE FUNERAL

WHOEVER comes to shroud me, do not harm,
Nor question much,
That subtle wreath of hair, which crowns my arm;
The mystery, the sign you must not touch;
For 'tis my outward soul,
Viceroy to that, which then to heaven being gone,
Will leave this to control
And keep these limbs, her provinces, from dissolution.

For if the sinewy thread my brain lets fall
Through every part
Can tie those parts, and make me one of all;
These hairs which upward grew, and strength and art
Have from a better brain,
Can better do 't; except she meant that I
By this should know my pain,
As prisoners then are manacled, when they're condemn'd to die.

Whate'er she meant by it, bury it with me,
For since I am
Love's martyr, it might breed idolatry,
If into other hands these relics came;
As 'twas humility
To afford to it all that a soul can do,
So 'tis some bravery,
That since you would save none of me, I bury some of you.

JOHN DONNE.

AIRE AND ANGELS

TWICE or thrice had I loved thee,
Before I knew thy face or name;
So in a voice, so in a shapeless flame,
Angels affect us oft, and worshipp'd be.
Still when, to where thou wert, I came,
Some lovely glorious nothing did I see.
But since my soul, whose child love is,
Takes limbs of flesh, and else could nothing do,
More subtle than the parent is
Love must not be, but take a body too;
And therefore what thou wert, and who,
I bid love ask, and now
That it assumes thy body, I allow,
And fix itself in thy lips, eyes, and brow.

Whilst thus to ballast love, I thought,
And so more steadily to have gone,
With wares that would sink admiration,
I saw I had love's pinnace overfraught,
Ev'ry thy hair for love to work upon
Is much too much, some fitter must be sought;
For, nor in nothing, nor in things
Extreme, and scatt'ring bright, can love inhere;
Then as an Angell, face and wings
Of aire, not pure as it, yet pure doth wear
So thy love may be my love's sphere;
Just such disparity
As is twixt Aire and Angells purity
'Twixt womens love and mens will ever be.

JOHN DONNE.

A FAREWELL

ONLY in my deep heart I love you, sweetest heart,
Many another vesture hath the soul, I pray
Call me not forth from this. If from the light I part
Only with clay I cling unto the clay.

And ah! my bright companion, you and I must go
Our ways, unfolding lonely glories, not our own,
Not from each other gathered, but an inward glow
Breathed by the Lone One to the seeker lone.

If for the heart's own sake we break the heart, we may
When the last ruby drop dissolves in diamond light
Meet in a deeper vesture in another day;
Until that dawn, dear heart, good-night, good-night.

A. E.

A SUPPLICATION

FORGET not yet the tried intent
Of such a truth as I have meant;
My great travail so gladly spent,
Forget not yet!

Forget not yet when first began
The weary life ye know, since whan
The suit, the service none tell can;
Forget not yet!

Forget not yet the great assays,
The cruel wrong, the scornful ways,
The painful patience in delays,
Forget not yet!

Forget not! O, forget not this,
How long ago hath been, and is
The mind that never meant amiss—
Forget not yet!

Forget not then thine own approved
The which so long hath thee so loved,
Whose steadfast faith yet never moved—
Forget not this!

SIR THOMAS WYAT.

SO shuts the marigold her leaves
At the departure of the sun;
So from the honeysuckle sheaves
The bee goes when the day is done;
So sits the turtle when she is but one,
And so all woe, as I since she is gone.

To some few birds kind Nature hath
Made all the summer as one day:
Which once enjoyed, cold winter's wrath
As night they sleeping pass away.
Those happy creatures are, that know not yet
The pain to be deprived or to forget.

I oft have heard me say there be
Some that with confidence profess
The helpful Art of Memory;
But could they teach Forgetfulness,
I'd learn; and try what further art could do
To make me love her, and forget her too. . . .

WILLIAM BROWNE.

LIGHTS OUT

I HAVE come to the borders of sleep,
The unfathomable deep
Forest where all must lose
Their way, however straight,
Or winding, soon or late;
They cannot choose.

Many a road and track
That, since the dawn's first crack,
Up to the forest brink,
Deceived the travellers
Suddenly now blurs,
And in they sink.

Here love ends,
Despair, ambition ends,
All pleasure and all trouble,
Although most sweet or bitter,
Here ends in sleep that is sweeter
Than tasks most noble.

There is not any book
Or face of dearest look
That I would not turn from now
To go into the unknown
I must enter and leave alone
I know not how.

The tall forest towers;
Its cloudy foliage lowers
Ahead, shelf above shelf;
Its silence I hear and obey
That I may lose my way
And myself.

EDWARD THOMAS.

GRIEF

A VALEDICTION OF WEEPING

LET me pour forth
  My tears before thy face, whilst I stay here,
For thy face coins them, and thy stamp they bear,
And by this mintage they are something worth.
            For thus they be
            Pregnant of thee;
Fruits of much grief they are, emblems of more;
When a tear falls, that thou fall'st which it bore;
So thou and I are nothing then, when on a divers shore.

            On a round ball
A workman, that hath copies by, can lay
An Europe, Afric, and an Asia,
And quickly make that, which was nothing, all.
            So doth each tear,
            Which thee doth wear,
A globe, yea world, by that impression grow,
Till thy tears mix'd with mine do overflow
This world, by waters sent from thee, my heaven
    dissolvéd so.

            O! more than moon,
Draw not up seas to drown me in thy sphere;
Weep me not dead, in thine arms, but forbear
To teach the sea, what it may do too soon;
            Let not the wind
            Example find
To do me more harm than it purposeth:
Since thou and I sigh one another's breath,
Whoe'er sighs most is cruellest, and hastes the other's
    death.

JOHN DONNE.

ON SUCH A DAY

SOME hang above the tombs,
  Some weep in empty rooms,
I, when the iris blooms,
    Remember.

I, when the cyclamen
Opens her buds again,
Rejoice a moment—then
    Remember.

MARY E. COLERIDGE.

AGE

THE AUTUMNAL

NO spring, nor summer beauty hath such grace
As I have seen in one autumnal face;
Young beauties force our love, and that 's a rape;
This doth but counsel, yet you cannot scape.
If 'twere a shame to love, here 'twere no shame;
Affection here take reverence's name.
Were her first years the Golden Age? that 's true,
But now they're gold oft tried, and ever new.
That was her torrid and inflaming time;
This is her tolerable tropic clime.
Fair eyes; who asks more heat than comes from hence,
He in a fever wishes pestilence.
Call not these wrinkles, graves; if graves they were,
They were Love's graves, for else he is nowhere.
Yet lies not Love dead here, but here doth sit,
Vow'd to this trench, like an anachorite.
And here, till hers, which must be his death, come,
He doth not dig a grave, but build a tomb.
Here dwells he; though he sojourn everywhere
In progress, yet his standing house is here;
Here, where still evening is, not noon, nor night;
Where no voluptuousness, yet all delight.
In all her words, unto all hearers fit,
You may at revels, you at council, sit.
This is love's timber; youth his underwood;
There he, as wine in June, enrages blood;
Which then comes seasonablest, when our taste
And appetite to other things is past.
Xerxes' strange Lydian love, the platane tree,
Was loved for age, none being so large as she;
Or else because, being young, nature did bless
Her youth with age's glory, barrenness.
If we love things long sought, age is a thing
Which we are fifty years in compassing;
If transitory things, which soon decay,
Age must be loveliest at the latest day.

But name not winter faces, whose skin 's slack,
Lank as an unthrift's purse, but a soul's sack;
Whose eyes seek light within, for all here 's shade;
Whose mouths are holes, rather worn out, than made;
Whose every tooth to a several place is gone,
To vex their souls at resurrection;
Name not these living deaths-heads unto me,
For these, not ancient, but antique be.
I hate extremes; yet I had rather stay
With tombs than cradles, to wear out a day.
Since such love's motion natural is, may still
My love descend, and journey down the hill,
Not panting after growing beauties; so
I shall ebb out with them who homeward go.

JOHN DONNE.

GHOSTS

SONG

I LISTEN for him through the rain,
And in the dusk of starless hours
I know he will return again;
Loth was he ever to forsake me.
He comes with glimmering of flowers
And stir of music to awake me.

Spirit of purity he stands
As once he lived, in charm and grace;
I may not hold him with these hands,
Nor bid him stay to heal my sorrow:
Only his fair unshadowed face
Abides with me until to-morrow.

SIEGFRIED SASSOON, 1910.

TWO LOVERS

I

WHEN thou must home to shades of underground,
And there arrived, a new admired guest,
The beauteous spirits do engirt thee round,
White Iope, blithe Helen, and the rest,
To hear the stories of thy finished love
From that smooth tongue whose music hell can move;

Then wilt thou speak of banqueting delights,
Of masques and revels which sweet youth did make,
Of tourneys and great challenges of knights,
And all these triumphs for thy beauty's sake:
When thou hast told these honours done to thee,
Then tell, O tell, how thou didst murder me.

THOMAS CAMPION.

II

OH! Death will find me, long before I tire
  Of watching you; and swing me suddenly
Into the shade and loneliness and mire
  Of the last land! There, waiting patiently,

One day, I think, I'll feel a cool wind blowing,
  See a slow light across the Stygian tide,
And hear the Dead about me stir, unknowing,
  And tremble. And I shall know that you have died,

And watch you, a broad-browed and smiling dream,
  Pass, light as ever, through the lightless host,
Quietly ponder, start, and sway, and gleam—
  Most individual and bewildering ghost—

And turn, and toss your brown delightful head,
Amusedly, among the ancient Dead.

RUPERT BROOKE.

MISTRESS FELL

"WHOM seek you here, sweet Mistress Fell?"
"One who loved me passing well.
Dark his eye, wild his face—
Stranger, if in this lonely place
Bide such an one, then, prythee, say
I am come here to-day."

"Many his like, Mistress Fell?"
"I did not look, so cannot tell.
Only this I surely know,
When his voice called me, I must go;
Touched me his fingers, and my heart
Leapt at the sweet pain's smart."

"Why did he leave you, Mistress Fell?"
"Magic laid its dreary spell.—
Stranger, he was fast asleep;
Into his dream I tried to creep;
Called his name, soft was my cry:
He answered—not one sigh.

"The flower and the thorn are here;
Falleth the night-dew, cold and clear;
Out of her bower the bird replies,
Mocking the dark with ecstasies,
See how the earth's green grass doth grow,
Praising what sleeps below!

"Thus have they told me. And I come,
As flies the wounded wild-bird home.
Not tears I give; but all that he
Clasped in his arms, sweet charity;
All that he loved—to him I bring
For a close whispering."

WALTER DE LA MARE.

GOD AND MAN

ADAM lay ibounden,
  Bounden in a bond;
Four thousand winter
  Thoght he not too long;
And all was for an appil,
  An appil that he tok,
As clerkes finden
  Wreten in here book.
Ne haddé the appil také ben,
  The appil taken ben,
Ne haddé never our lady
  A ben hevené quene.
Blesséd be the time
  That appil také was.
Therefore we moun singen
  "Deo gracias."

Carol from the Sloane MS.

IF thou could'st empty all thyself of self,
   Like to a shell dishabited,
Then might He find thee on the ocean shelf
   And say: "This is not dead,"
   And fill thee with Himself instead.

But thou art all replete with very thou,
   And hast such shrewd activity,
That when He comes He says: "This is enow
   Unto itself—'twere better let it be,
   It is so small and full, there is no room for Me."

T. E. BROWNE.

THE OBSEQUIES

SINCE dying for me, thou didst crave no more
Than common pay,
Some few true tears, and those shed for
My own ill way;
With a cheap, plain remembrance still
Of thy sad death,
Because forgetfulness would kill
Even life's own breath:
I were most foolish and unkinde
In my own sense,
Should I not ever bear in minde,
If not thy mighty love, my own defense,
Therefore those loose delights and lusts, which here
Men call good chear,
I will, close girt and tyed,
For mourning sack-cloth wear all mortified.

Not but that mourners too can have
Rich weeds and shrouds;
But some wore *White* ev'n in thy grave,
And joy, like light, shines oft in clouds:
But thou, who didst man's whole life earn,
Doest so invite and woo me still,
That to be merry I want skill,
And time to learn.
Besides, those kerchiefs sometimes shed
To make me brave,
I cannot find, but where thy head
Was once laid for me in thy grave.
Thy grave! To which my thoughts shall move
Like bees in storms unto their hive;
That from the murd'ring world's false love
Thy death may keep my soul alive.

HENRY VAUGHAN.

HYMN

SPIRIT of God! descend upon my heart!
  Wean it from earth, through all its pulses move,
Stoop to my weakness, mighty as Thou art,
  And make me love Thee as I ought to love.

I ask no dream, no prophet ecstasies,
  No sudden rending of the veil of clay;
No angel visitant, no opening skies,
  But take the dimness of my soul away.

Hast Thou not bid us love Thee, God and King?
  All, all Thine own—soul, heart, and strength and
    mind;
I see Thy Cross—there teach my heart to cling:
  O let me seek Thee, and O let me find.

Teach me to feel that Thou art always nigh;
  Teach me the struggles of the soul to bear;
To check the rising doubt, the rebel sigh;
  Teach me the patience of unanswered prayer.

Teach me to love Thee as Thine angels love,
  One holy passion filling all my frame;
The baptism of the heaven-descended Dove,
  My heart an altar, and Thy love the flame.

DR. CROLY.

DEATH

THOUGH since thy first sad entrance by
Just Abel's blood,
'Tis now six thousand years well nigh,
And still thy sov'rainty holds good;
Yet by none art thou understood.

We talk and name thee with much ease,
As a tryed thing;
And every one can slight his lease,
As if it ended in a Spring,
Which shades and bowers doth rent-free bring.

To thy dark land these heedless go.
But there was One,
Who search'd it quite through to and fro,
And then, returning like the sun,
Discover'd all that there is done.

And since His death we throughly see
All thy dark way;
Thy shades but thin and narrow be,
Which his first looks will quickly fray:
Mists make but triumphs for the day.

As harmless violets, which give
Their virtues here
For salves and syrups while they live,
Do after calmly disappear,
And neither grieve, repine, nor fear:

So dye his servants; and as sure
Shall they revive.
Then let not dust your eyes obscure,
But lift them up, where still alive,
Though fled from you, their spirits hive.

HENRY VAUGHAN.

EPITAPH

HERE lies, but seven years old, our little maid:
Once of the darkness—oh! so sore afraid.
Light of the World—remember that small fear,
And when nor moon nor stars do shine—draw near!

WALTER DE LA MARE.

THE PULLEY

WHEN God at first made man,
    Having a glass of blessings standing by,
"Let us," said He, "pour on him all we can;
    Let the world's riches which disperséd lie,
Contract into a span."

So strength first made a way;
    Then beauty flowed; then wisdom, honour, pleasure;
When almost all was out, God made a stay;
    Perceiving that alone, of all his treasure,
Rest in the bottom lay.

"For if I should," said He,
    "Bestow this jewel also on my creature,
He would adore my gifts instead of me,
    And rest in nature, not the God of nature—
So both should losers be.

"Yet let him keep the rest—
    But keep them with repining restlessness—
Let him be rich and weary; that, at least,
    If goodness lead him not, yet weariness
May toss him to my breast."

GEORGE HERBERT.

ANOTHER tattered rhymster in the ring,
With but the old plea to the sneering schools,
That on him too, some secret night in spring
Came the old frenzy of a hundred fools.

To make some thing: the old want dark and deep,
The thirst of men, the hunger of the stars,
Since it tinged even the Eternal's sleep,
With monstrous dreams of trees and towns and wars.

When all He made for the first time He saw,
Scattering stars as misers shake their pelf.
Then in the last strange wrath broke His own law,
And made a graven image of Himself.

GILBERT CHESTERTON.

SPIT in my face, you Jews, and pierce my side,
Buffet, and scoff, scourge and crucify me,
For I have sinn'd, and sinn'd, and only He,
Who could do no iniquity, hath died.
But by my death can not be satisfied
My sins, which pass the Jews' impiety.
They kill'd once an inglorious man, but I
Crucify Him daily, being now glorified.
O let me then His strange love still admire;
Kings pardon, but He bore our punishment;
And Jacob came clothed in vile harsh attire,
But to supplant, and with gainful intent;
God clothed Himself in vile man's flesh, that so
He might be weak enough to suffer woe.

JOHN DONNE.

FOUR OF SHAKESPEARE'S SONNETS

I

SOME glory in their birth, some in their skill,
Some in their wealth, some in their body's force;
Some in their garments, though new-fangled ill;
Some in their hawks and hounds, some in their horse;
And every humour hath his adjunct pleasure,
Wherein it finds a joy above the rest:
But these particulars are not my measure;
All these I better in one general best.
Thy love is better than high birth to me,
Richer than wealth, prouder than garments' cost,
Of more delight than hawks or horses be;
And having thee, of all men's pride I boast:
Wretched in this alone, that thou mayst take
All this away and me most wretched make.

II

SO am I as the rich, whose blessèd key
Can bring him to his sweet up-lockèd treasure,
The which he will not every hour survey,
For blunting the fine point of seldom pleasure.
Therefore are feasts so solemn and so rare,
Since, seldom coming, in the long year set,
Like stones of worth they thinly placed are,
Or captain jewels in the carcanet.
So is the time that keeps you as my chest,
Or as the wardrobe which the robe doth hide,
To make some special instant special blest,
By new unfolding his imprison'd pride.
Blessed are you, whose worthiness gives scope,
Being had, to triumph, being lack'd, to hope.

III

THEN hate me when thou wilt ; if ever, now ;
Now, while the world is bent my deeds to cross,
Join with the spite of fortune, make me bow,
And do not drop in for an after-loss :
Ah, do not, when my heart hath 'scaped this sorrow,
Come in the rearward of a conquer'd woe ;
Give not a windy night a rainy morrow,
To linger out a purposed overthrow.
If thou wilt leave me, do not leave me last,
When other petty griefs have done their spite,
But in the onset come : so shall I taste
At first the very worst of fortune's might ;
And other strains of woe, which now seem woe,
Compared with loss of thee will not seem so.

IV

NOT mine own fears, nor the prophetic soul
Of the wide world dreaming on things to come,
Can yet the lease of my true love control,
Supposed as forfeit to a confined doom.
The mortal moon hath her eclipse endured,
And the sad augurs mock their own presage ;
Incertainties now crown themselves assured,
And peace proclaims olives of endless age.
Now with the drops of this most balmy time
My love looks fresh, and Death to me subscribes,
Since, spite of him, I'll live in this poor rhyme,
While he insults o'er dull and speechless tribes:
And thou in this shalt find thy monument,
When tyrants' crests and tombs of brass are spent.

NINE SONGS

I

Lully, lully, lully, lulley,
The faucon hath borne my mate away.

HE bare him up, he bare him down,
He bare him into an orchard brown.

In that orchard there was a halle,
That was hangèd with purpill and pall.

And in that hall there was a bede,
It was hangèd with gold so rede.

And in that bed there lithe a knight,
His woundès bleding day and night.

By that bede side kneleth a may,
And she wepeth both night and day.

And by that bede side there stondeth a stone,
Corpus Christi wreten there on.

Fifteenth Century Carol.

II

ROBIN GOODFELLOW

AND can the physician make sick men well?
And can the magician a fortune divine?
Without lily, germander and sops-in-wine,
With sweet-brier
And bon-fire
And strawberry wire
And columbine.

With in-and-out, in-and-out, round as a ball,
With hither and thither, as straight as a line,
With lily, germander and sops-in-wine,
With sweet-brier
And bon-fire
And strawberry wire
And columbine.

When Saturn did live, there livèd no poor;
The king and the beggar with roots did dine,
With lily, germander and sops-in-wine,
With sweet-brier
And bon-fire
And strawberry wire
And columbine.

With in-and-out, in-and-out, round as a ball,
With hither and thither, as straight as a line,
With lily, germander and sops-in-wine,
With sweet-brier
And bon-fire
And strawberry wire
And columbine.

ANON. 1628.

III

NOT, Celia, that I juster am
Or better than the rest;
For I would change each hour like them,
Were not my heart at rest.

But I am tied to very thee
By every thought I have;
Thy face I only care to see,
Thy heart I only crave.

All that in woman is adored
In thy dear self I find;
For the whole sex can but afford
The handsome and the kind.

Why then should I seek further store,
And still make love anew?
When change itself can give no more
'Tis easy to be true.

SIR CHARLES SEDLEY.

IV

CORONACH

HE is gone on the mountain,
He is lost to the forest,
Like a summer-dried fountain,
When our need was sorest.
The font reappearing
From the raindrops shall borrow,
But to us comes no cheering,
To Duncan no morrow!

The hand of the reaper
Takes the ears that are hoary,
But the voice of the weeper
Wails manhood in glory.
The autumn winds rushing
Waft the leaves that are serest,
But our flower was in flushing
When blighting was nearest.

Fleet foot on the correi,
Sage counsel in cumber,
Red hand in the foray,
How sound is thy slumber!
Like the dew on the mountain,
Like the foam on the river
Like the bubble on the fountain,
Thou art gone, and for ever!

SIR WALTER SCOTT.

V

I HAD a dove and the sweet dove died;
  And I have thought it died of grieving:
O, what could it grieve for? Its feet were tied,
  With a silken thread of my own hand's weaving;
Sweet little red feet! why should you die—
Why should you leave me, sweet bird! why?
You liv'd alone in the forest-tree,
Why, pretty thing! would you not live with me?
I kiss's you oft and gave you white peas;
Why not live sweetly, as in the green trees?

JOHN KEATS.

VI

THE autumn skies are flushed with gold
And fair and bright the rivers run;
These are but streams of winter cold
And painted mists that quench the sun.

In secret boughs no sweet birds sing,
In secret boughs no birds can shroud;
These are but leaves that take to wing
And wintry winds that pipe so loud.

'Tis not trees' shade, but cloudy glooms
That on the cheerless valleys fall,
The flowers are in their grassy tombs
And tears of dew are on them all.

THOMAS HOOD.

VII

TO ONE IN PARADISE

THOU wast that all to me, love,
For which my soul did pine—
A green isle in the sea, love,
A fountain and a shrine,
All wreathed with fairy fruits and flowers,
And all the flowers were mine.

Ah, dream, too bright to last!
Ah, starry hope, that didst arise
But to be overcast!
A voice from out the future cries,
"On! On!"—but o'er the past
(Dim gulf!) my spirit, hovering lies,
Mute, motionless, agast!

For alas, alas, with me,
The light of life is o'er
"No more—no more—no more—"
(Such language holds the solemn sea
To the sands upon the shore)
Shall bloom the thunder-blasted tree
Or the stricken eagle soar!

And all my days are trances,
And all my nightly dreams
Are where thy dark eye glances,
And where thy footstep gleams;
In what ethereal dances,
By what eternal streams.

EDGAR ALLAN POE.

VIII

ASPIRATION

I ENVY not the sun
  His lavish light;
But O to be the one
  Pale orb of night,
In silence and alone
Communing with mine own!

I envy not the rain
  That freshens all
The parching hill and plain;
  But O the small
Night-dewdrop now to be,
My noonday flower, for thee!

JOHN BANNISTER TABB.

IX

AUTUMN

THERE is wind where the rose was;
Cold rain where sweet grass was;
And clouds like sheep
Stream o'er the steep
Grey skies where the lark was.

Nought gold where your hair was;
Nought warm where your hand was;
But phantom, forlorn,
Beneath the thorn,
Your ghost where your face was.

Sad winds where your voice was;
Tears, tears, where my heart was;
And ever with me
Child, ever with me,
Silence where hope was.

WALTER DE LA MARE.